SUPER SKATERS

World Figure Skating Stars

STEVE MILTON

CRESCENT
BOOKS

This 1997 edition is published by Crescent Books,
a division of Random House Value Publishing, Inc.,
40 Engelhard Avenue, Avenel, New Jersey 07001.

Crescent Books and colophon are registered trademarks of
Random House Value Publishing, Inc.

Random House
New York • Toronto • London • Sydney • Auckland
http://www.randomhouse.com/

Illustrations: Angela Vaculik
Printed and bound in Canada

Library of Congress Cataloging-in-Publication Data

Milton, Steve.
    [Super skaters II]
    Super skaters : world figure skating stars / Steve Milton.
       p.   cm.
    Originally published: Super skaters. Toronto : Key Porter,
c1996.
    ISBN 0-517-18482-6 (hard)
    1. Skaters–Biography.   2. Skating.   I. Title.
GV850.A2M55   1997
796.91'2'0922–dc20
[B]   96-35848
                                   CIP

8 7 6 5 4 3 2 1

From bone blades to rock stars

As the Winter Olympics figure skating competition drew to a close, Don Knight flipped off his television set and shook his head in amazement.

"Unbelievable what these kids can do now!" exclaimed the former Canadian champion. "How they can jump, how they're dressed, the variety of music they skate to."

For two weeks, Don had been watching the 1994 Olympics from Lillehammer, Norway. It was a much different scene from the 1964 Olympics, where he had been one of the world's best skaters.

"In our day, everyone skated to classical music, *everyone*," Don recalled. "And I remember the 1966 World Championships. School figures were held in an outside rink. It started to snow, and you couldn't make your skates move over the clumps where the judges had walked. One night it rained during the pairs freeskating. It was ludicrous. A year or so after that, they moved everything indoors for good.

"We had compulsory figures then, and they don't have them now. And our costumes were much different. The dress that Peggy Fleming wore [to win at the 1968 Olympics] — you wouldn't see a girl dressed like that even for practice today. Men all wore the same kind of suit, buttoned up to the neck, with a tie. It was more formal and regimented. We looked like waiters in some fancy dining room."

The 1994 Olympics saw skaters dressed in karate outfits, Italian peasant clothes, movie star garb, and glittery costumes costing several thousand dollars each. Those skaters were seen on television by hundreds of millions of people around the world. They were described and interviewed by announcers who knew everything about them.

"These kids are like rock stars now," says Gerri Walbert, editor of *Blades On Ice*, an American skating magazine. "They're recognized everywhere. They're on TV all the time. They've all got their own fan clubs."

"Yeah, it is like being a rock star, only scaled down a bit," marvels Kurt Browning, four-time world champion from Canada. "There are moments when you really feel like one. But I'm glad it's only moments, because you like to be able to walk down the street and not be mobbed."

Skating's earliest years

Today's figure skating superstars have come a long way since Don Knight's years as a championship contender three decades ago. Just think how much further they've come from the earliest moments of the sport.

It's impossible to say who invented the first skate or where and when it first touched the ice. But historians believe that it may have been more than 40 centuries ago. By that time people were already trying to get extra help moving on frozen surfaces by strapping long pieces of animal bone to their feet. One such pair of "blades" is on display in the city of Berne, Switzerland. Scientists have determined it is probably about 4000 years old.

For people in northern climates, skating has for centuries provided an enjoyable way to deal with the cold and ice of winter. Historians have found evidence that metal skates were in use by the 1300s in Holland. Because metal skates cut more deeply into the ice than bone skates, they allowed the skater to move more quickly and smoothly. It was very important for the Dutch to have a way of traveling on their vast network of canals which, of course, froze during the winter.

As more and more people in Europe and North America discovered the pleasures of skating, they began to skate together on ponds and lakes. The first skating club in the world, the Edinburgh Skating Club in chilly Scotland, came into being around 1650. To join the club, you had to be able to skate in a circle on one foot, then on the other foot, then jump over a pile of three hats. Perhaps these tricky exercises could be considered the first skating competition.

As skating's popularity grew, the equipment improved. In the early years, most blades were attached to normal street boots with leather straps. But by 1750, the British had "invented" the figure skate. A longer blade, which ran past the heel of the boot, was created. The blade was curved and had a groove in it. Turning and backward skating — so essential to the sport we know today — were no longer so difficult. Soon, skate blades were attached to their own special boots.

Skating in the 1800s and early 1900s

By the 1800s, there were skating clubs all over Europe. They began springing up in North America as well, starting in Philadelphia in 1849. The New York Skating Club was founded in 1860. Because much of the skating was done on frozen rivers, members had to carry rope so that they could help in case the ice broke and someone fell through. North America's first covered rinks were built in Canada, in Quebec City and Montreal.

An 1863 drawing of an awards ceremony held after a skating match at a Toronto, Ontario, rink. *Metropolitan Toronto Library*

With organized clubs came more regular practice and the development of more intricate moves. An idea was born that continues to this day — the club carnival. It allowed skaters of all abilities to put on fancy costumes and be part of a show. The tradition of club carnivals eventually led to professional shows such as Ice Capades, Walt Disney on Ice, and Holiday on Ice. Most of today's superstars encountered their first big audiences at club carnivals.

Early North American skaters had a rather formal style that proved too stiff for more creative types. Jackson Haines, an expressive American skater of the early years, became very successful in Europe, skating his fancy "International Style" in exhibitions for kings and queens. One of his students, Canadian Louis Rubenstein, helped organize the groups that later became the Canadian Figure Skating Association and the United States Figure Skating Association. International style skating was what we today call "freeskating." It included jumps and spins and fancy footwork. Those parts of skating are officially called "elements," but skaters refer to them as "tricks." Skaters make comments such as "I've got a double Axel, a flying-sit-spin, and a few other tricks in my program."

During the 1800s, many skaters, particularly in Europe, were becoming skilled at carving detailed designs in the ice. They would form figure-eights, stars, brackets, and loops. They could even use their skates to sign their own names. If they had enough time and smooth ice, they could write you a letter!

The skaters' tracings became known as figures. They remained an important part of skating until just a few years ago. People felt you weren't a "real" figure skater unless you excelled at figures, also called "school figures" or "compulsory figures."

Figures, therefore, formed a large part of early championships. The first international meet, in Vienna in 1882, required skaters to do 23 different figures and a freeskating routine that lasted four minutes. The first World Championships were held in St. Petersburg, Russia, in 1896. Germany's Gilbert Fuchs won.

For a number of years, championship skating was considered a man's sport. However, in 1902, Madge Syers of Great Britain shocked the authorities by entering the four-person competition. She finished second to longtime champion Ulrich Salchow. The officials, all men, quickly decided to ban women from the championships! But a separate women's event was set up in 1906, and when skating was included in the 1908 Summer Olympics (indoors, of course), Madge Syers won the first women's gold medal.

Skating was included in one last Summer Olympics (1920) before a separate Winter Olympic Games was started in 1924. Figure skating was one of its main attractions, as it is today.

Those first Winter Olympics introduced the world to a blonde, blue-eyed Norwegian. She was only 11 at the time, but she would eventually change the world of figure skating. Sonja Henie finished last among the eight competitors, but she had tried jumps and sit-spins that only men had done previously. Unlike the other women, who wore heavy ankle-length skirts, Sonja wore short skirts that allowed her to do more difficult tricks on the ice.

By 1927 Sonja Henie was world champion. She won ten straight titles, the most ever won by a woman, and three Olympic championships. Most importantly, she took figure skating away from a small privileged group, made up mostly of men, and brought it to a worldwide audience. A dramatic figure on and off the ice, Sonja was the first to use drama and dance in her skating performances. Her fourth world championship, in New York in 1930, started a huge figure skating boom in the United States and Canada. Hollywood began planning movies with Sonja in a starring role. She made 11 movies in all and became the first female athlete to make a million dollars during her career.

Today's competitions

Although figure skaters spend up to six hours a day training for their sport, there are actually very few competitions in a year.

The season usually opens in the autumn with the fall internationals. There are several competitions for the best skaters to choose from. Among them are Skate Canada, Skate America, Trophée Lalique in France, Nation's Cup in Germany, and NHK Trophy in Japan. As well, a number of other competitions are open to up-and-coming skaters. They include Prague Skate, Blue Swords, and Coupe des Alpes.

The fall internationals are used to test out new programs in front of judges and to compare a skater's development with that of other skaters in his or her event. Usually no more than two or three of the world's top skaters in each event are present at any one fall international. But that's changing as these events become more important.

In late December or early January, skaters begin qualifying for their country's national championships. In the leading skating nations such as Canada and the United States, the qualifying involves regional and divisional championships. The top finishers advance to the national championships.

From the nationals the top one, two, or three skaters advance to the World Championships (and Olympics in an Olympic year). The World Championships and Olympics figure skating are run by the International Skating Union, based in Davos, Switzerland.

The number of skaters each country is allowed to send to the Worlds is determined by the results of the previous year. If a country wins a medal in dance, men's singles, or women's singles, it has three entries in that event the following year. In pairs, a top-five finish earns three entries for the following year. A finish from fourth to tenth (sixth to tenth in pairs) qualifies two of that country's skaters for the next year. Otherwise, each country has one entry in the World Championships. If there are too many entries, a qualifying round is held just before the World Championships to reduce the number of contestants.

European countries have an extra event, the European Championships, between their nationals and the World Championships. The European Championships, however, are not used as a qualifying round for Worlds. They're just another chance for skaters to be seen by international judges.

Amateur or professional?

In the early 1930s, Sonja Henie could not make her million dollars while she was still an amateur skater. There were strict rules against accepting money for skating performances. If you did, you were no longer considered an amateur and could not enter the World or Olympic championships.

Sonja Henie performs a forward spiral in 1943 in Hollywood, California, where she made a number of movies. *Canapress*

When Canada's Barbara Ann Scott became the first North American to win a world championship in 1947, her home town of Ottawa was so proud that it held a parade and gave her a canary yellow convertible. However, the head of the International Olympic Committee said that if Barbara Ann accepted the car, she would have to give up her medal and also be banned from the Olympics. Reluctantly, she refused the convertible.

What could Sonja and other amateur championship skaters do if they wanted to make money and still keep skating? Skating had become so popular that audiences were willing to pay to watch it. The occasional professional skating show had been around since the first one at the New York Hippodrome in 1915. But now many more sprang up. Starting with Sonja, a number of amateur champions turned professional and were signed to "headline" such shows. Skaters could also "turn professional" by coaching other skaters for a fee.

The amateur skaters have always been more famous than the professional skaters (other than the legendary Sonja) because they are written about in the newspapers and shown on TV at the national championships and Olympics. About ten years ago, amateurs were allowed to start "trust funds." This let them accept money for skating, but it would be saved for them until they turned professional. Soon amateurs such as Canada's Kurt Browning were making as much money as professional skaters. Some had their own TV shows or were in commercials. They were also allowed to skate in touring shows with professionals. These shows brought the best of both amateur and professional worlds together.

"Skating gets so much exposure now," says 1992 Olympic winner Kristi Yamaguchi, now a professional. "It's on TV almost every weekend and amateurs skate with pros. In that way, younger skaters are learning earlier in their careers what skating in front of TV and big audiences is like."

For instance, when Michelle Kwan was just 13, she won the U.S. Olympic Festival in front of 25,691 people, the largest crowd ever to attend a figure skating competition.

The shift from compulsory figures to freeskating

As the line between pro and amateur skaters blurred, amateur skating improved and the rules changed. People began questioning why figures played such a big role in men's and women's singles competitions. For more than 75 years, they had counted more in the final standing than freeskating had.

However, it was freeskating that the audiences wanted to see. After World War II, American and Canadian skaters began to win more championships. (Skating had all but stopped in Europe during the war, but North Americans were able to continue practicing and competing.) With the rise of the North Americans came a greater interest in freeskating and the "tricks" that went with it. Starting with the fabulous American Dick Button in the late 1940s and early 1950s, skaters began trying more daring stunts, particularly jumps.

The exciting freeskating became increasingly popular. When Austrian Beatrix Schuba, a terrible freeskater, won the 1972 world championship because she was so far ahead on points after compulsory figures, changes were quickly made. The short program was introduced, requiring skaters to show how well they can perform different elements (spins, jumps, combinations, and footwork). Figures were reduced in importance.

Fans still wondered why compulsory figures, which weren't shown on TV and which few people came to watch, could influence who won the championship. Without figures, for instance, Canadian Brian Orser, the 1987 world champion, would also have won the 1984 Olympics and three other world titles.

Over the years the compulsory figures declined in value from 60 percent to 20 percent of the total mark. After the 1990 World Championships, they were finally eliminated. Many countries still require junior and novice skaters to do figures. But senior competitors no longer have to spend long, tiring, and expensive hours practicing figure-eights on the ice.

The elimination of figures has helped increase the popularity of skating even more. In North America alone, more than a quarter of a million people belong to figure skating associations — 180,000 in Canada and 100,000 in the United States.

Now competitive skaters just do the technical (or short) program, worth a third of the final mark and a freeskate (long) program worth the other two-thirds.

Famous firsts

Unlike some sports, which can drown you with statistics, figure skating has not done a very good job in recording its historic moments. The International Skating Union, which governs amateur competitions around the world, does not officially recognize pioneers in jumping. Perhaps that is partly because figure skating is a sport that depends less upon who does the jump first and more upon who does it best.

There was often a debate about whether a jump had actually been completed. For instance, Canada's

Vern Taylor is given credit for the first triple Axel. But some say the jump wasn't done well enough to count, even though he landed it on one foot, the usual standard for deciding whether a jump is successful. Vern did a small turn, called a three-turn, coming out of the jump, according to respected skating official and historian Ben Wright of Boston. "I'd prefer to think it was Brian Orser who did the first triple Axel, because he did it right." Similarly, many skating fans think Surya Bonaly of France was the first woman to do a quadruple jump. But skating officials felt her final turn was done not in the air but on the ice. So it's generally considered that no quad has yet been done by a woman.

Everyone does agree on one thing. To be a "first," a jump has to be performed at a major competition, such as a national, fall international, World or Olympic championships. Landing it in practice or at a show does not count. Here are a few of the most important "firsts," as recognized by most skating insiders.

FIRSTS — MEN

- **First Double Axel: Dick Button (U.S.A.) in St. Moritz, 1948**
- **First Triple Jump (a triple loop): Dick Button (U.S.A.) in Oslo, 1952**
- **First Triple Lutz: Donald Jackson (Canada) in Prague, 1962**
- **First Triple Axel: Vern Taylor (Canada) in Ottawa, 1978**
- **First Quadruple Jump (a quadruple toe loop): Kurt Browning (Canada) in Budapest, 1988**
- **First Quadruple Jump Combination (a quad toe loop/double toe loop): Elvis Stojko (Canada) in Munich, 1991**

FIRSTS — WOMEN

- **First Double Jump (a double Salchow): Cecilia Colledge (Great Britain) in Berlin, 1936**
- **First Triple Jump (a triple Salchow): Jana Mrazkova (Czechoslovakia) in Colorado Springs, 1959**
- **First Triple Lutz: Denise Biellmann (Switzerland) in Strasbourg, 1978**
- **First Triple Axel: Midori Ito (Japan) in Paris, 1989**
- **First Quadruple Jump: Not yet accomplished**

Pairs skating and ice dancing

By 1908 pairs skating was included in the World Championships, but it was not until 1952 that ice dancing was allowed into the Championships. That brought the number of figure skating divisions to the four we have today: women's singles, men's singles, pairs, and ice dancing.

Pairs skaters, like men's and women's singles, skate a short and a long program. Ice dancers, however, retain their version of the compulsory figures: two compulsory dances, each worth 10 percent of the final mark. Every couple does the same two dances. Ice dancers have an original program, worth 30 percent. In it, every couple must skate to the same kind of music but interpret it in their own way. The free dance, like the freeskate, can include whatever the skaters wish. It's worth 50 percent of the final mark.

Many people confuse ice dancing with pairs skating. To get a better idea of the difference, consider the Canadian champions in those two events.

Victor Kraatz spends most of his program holding onto his dance partner, Shae-Lynn Bourne. He swings her around, supports the back of her head in a very dangerous move, dances cheek to cheek with her while doing precise footwork ... but he almost never lets go of her. Pairs champion Lloyd Eisler, on the other hand, tosses his partner Isabelle Brasseur 15 feet (4.5 m) through the air backward in a throw-double-Axel. He flings her over his head in their triple lateral twist and catches her on the way down. Isabelle and Lloyd do side-by-side double-Axel jumps some 5 feet (1.5 m) apart.

Pairs skating emphasizes unison in jumps, spins, and footwork. It appeals to audiences because of its daring throws and lifts. Ice dancing highlights rhythm, harmony, dramatic interpretation of the music, and precise steps. Partners must not separate except for the brief moments necessary to change positions.

In both ice dancing and pairs, it's important that both partners be committed. "You spend more time with your partner than you do with your parents or with your girlfriend or boyfriend," says Lloyd Eisler.

It's helpful if the partners get along well, but it's not absolutely necessary. There have been many successful pairs who could not stand each other! But usually that will lead to a breakup in time, as it did with former American champions Rocky Marval and Calla Urbanski.

Sometimes the partners get along really well. Lloyd and Isabelle, for instance, were boyfriend and girlfriend for two years before they decided they were spending too much time together, and it might be affecting their skating. So they started dating other people. And American Todd Sand left his pairs partner Natasha Kuchiki, with whom he finished sixth at the 1992 Olympics, because he fell in love with Jenni Meno and wanted to skate with her. They made the 1994 Olympic team and skated brilliantly to finish fifth. Many of the great Russian pairs, such as Ekaterina Gordeeva and Sergei Grinkov, are married couples.

Paying the bills

Skating is demanding, rewarding, difficult ... and also expensive. American dance champions Elizabeth Punsalan and Jerod Swallow are another married couple. Just before the national championships in 1994, they outlined for a Detroit newspaper just how much it cost to keep themselves skating. Elizabeth and Jerod estimated that ice rentals, costume and equipment purchases, coaches' and choreographers' fees, travel budgets, and food and lodging costs ran up a bill of about $55,000 per year.

Some countries, such as the United States, Canada, France, and sometimes Russia, help their top skaters with some or all of those costs. For example, about one-third of Elizabeth and Jerod's expenses were covered by grants. They had to raise the rest of the money themselves. For skaters still trying to reach the upper level, even less financial help is given by the national skating associations.

So it was a welcome relief ten years ago when amateur skaters were permitted to earn money in ways that had been closed to them for many years. If Barbara Ann Scott were competing today, she could accept that yellow convertible.

A sport that's changing fast

"Just look at the way skating has changed even in my time," says Kurt Browning, who won four world titles between 1989 and 1994. "The short program is different. The figures are gone — that's the big one.... You can skate in shows with professionals more than you could when I started.

"We have a tour that goes around Canada, and the first one we took just went to a few little towns. Now we take our tour into the biggest cities and fill National Hockey League arenas. Figure skating is huge, comparatively, to when I started, which wasn't that long ago."

Dick Button, the first American world champion, is the man who introduced so many jumps and exciting moves to the sport from 1948 to 1952. He says that "the biggest changes are there are no figures now, and there is very little difference between pros and amateurs."

There's so little difference, in fact, that professionals were allowed to come back to the Olympics (for the first time) in February 1994 at Lillehammer, Norway.

Amateurs go on tour more than they used to and professionals take part in more competitions than they used to. And the "tricks" the professionals do every night in their tours are closer to what the amateurs do in competition than they were in Sonja Henie's or Dick Button's time.

"Brian Boitano and Scott Hamilton really pulled pro skating to a higher level because they kept all of their tricks up," sighs Kristi Yamaguchi. "We still have to do triple Lutzes and triple flips on tour. We laugh about it because it must have been so easy way back when, when you didn't have to do that stuff as a pro."

Now pros do have to do "that stuff," and amateurs also have to do more. Figure skating has become so competitive that jumps considered almost impossible just a few years ago are now absolutely necessary to win an Olympic or World medal.

A perfect example of the technical demands of today's figure skating was the men's freeskate final of the 1995 World Championships in Birmingham, England. American Todd Eldredge fell on an important triple Axel—the hardest triple there is—early in the program. He knew that he could not win a medal without making that jump, so he threw in an extra one near the end of his program, and landed it. That change was good enough to put Todd into first place before Elvis Stojko skated.

Elvis knew Todd had skated well and that he needed to skate better than the American to win. So at the end of *his* program, he added an extra turn to a planned triple-Lutz double-toe jump combination, turning it into a triple-triple. That was enough to let Elvis win the title. "It was amazing," said Todd.

The next year, 1996, it was Todd's turn. He was one of only a few skaters to do a triple-Axel triple-toe combination in the short program and was second behind Ilya Kulik of Russia, who also did that combination. But in the long program, Todd had two triple-triple combinations and Ilya had only one. So Todd won the World Championships. "So now I know that I can't turn a triple-triple into a triple," Ilya said afterward.

If the skating is much more difficult today, the rewards are also much greater. In order to compete with the professionals, the International Skating Union is now paying prize money for its major competitions, including the Worlds. Winners of each event get $50,000.

And the top five fall internationals have been grouped together into a tour called the Champions Series. The top six finishers in the series then compete in a championship final, with the winners taking home $50,000. It has become the third most important skating event in the world, behind the Olympic Games and Worlds.

Skating has become one of the most popular sports in the world. A survey in the United States, for example, showed that women's singles, men's singles, dance, and pairs ranked second, third, fourth, and fifth in overall popularity, trailing only professional football.

Figure skaters have become ... superstars.

Oksana Baiul

To say she came out of nowhere does not even begin to tell the story of how the fragile-looking, fawn-eyed Oksana Baiul exploded onto the world figure skating scene.

She was unknown outside her practice rink in Odessa, Ukraine, until she won the silver medal at the European Championships in 1993. A month later, 15-year-old Oksana was world champion, the youngest since Sonja Henie won in 1927 at age 14. The following year, 1994, Oksana won Olympic gold.

As Olympic champion, Oksana was the winner of the most publicized women's skating final in Olympic history. Her victory over American Nancy Kerrigan at the Lillehammer Games was gained by the slimmest possible margin: one mark on one judge's card. Oksana's incredible artistry broke the tie.

It took all of Oksana's charm and delicate grace to triumph over the other skaters. But it took her strength and determination to triumph over a serious accident the day before the freeskate final. During a practice, she and German champion Tanja Szewczenko collided. This resulted in injuries for both. Oksana suffered a three-stitch gash in her right leg and also wrenched her back. It was not certain until just before the freeskate whether she would be able to compete.

As a child, Oksana wanted to be a ballerina but was turned down by the ballet school. Instead, she was enrolled in skating. Her early love of dance is evident in her skating style. She lands fewer triple jumps than some of her toughest opponents, but makes up for it in a beautiful interpretation of her music. "You

see Oksana's inner soul out there," says American coach Kathy Case.

Bubbly and sassy on the ice, Oksana shows little of the sadness that was part of her earlier life. When she was an infant, in the city of Dnepropetrovsk, her father died in an accident. Then, when Oksana was 13, her mother died of cancer, leaving her an orphan. The next year, her coach left the country, to live in Canada. Oksana had to move 300 miles (480 km) to Odessa to work with coach Galina Zmievskaya, who also coached 1992 Olympic men's champion Viktor Petrenko. "God has taken away her family," says Galina. "But now the skating world is her family."

Oksana moved in with Galina. Viktor took a special interest in the talented but unknown skater from his homeland. Having turned professional, he began helping to pay many of Oksana's training expenses.

Viktor says, "I first saw her in the summer of 1992, and I knew she was something special. As a skater you can see right away when someone has it."

Oksana and Viktor continue to be close friends, and now Viktor, Galina and Oksana have all moved to the same town in the United States—Simsbury, Connecticut. In fact, Viktor is married to Galina's daughter.

But Oksana has not forgotten her native Ukraine. When she and Viktor receive stuffed animals or T-shirts from fans after a performance, they bundle them up and send them to an orphanage in Ukraine.

Oksana turned professional after the 1994 Olympics, and when skating officials gave professionals one last chance to return to amateur skating in 1995, she decided to stay pro. She has won several major professional competitions and often skates with Viktor on tour.

Oksana usually takes longer than most skaters to start her program after her name has been called. "I try to concentrate," she explains of the delay. "I listen to my skates. When they can start, I can start."

Those skates must know what they're talking about because it's been more than 65 years since anyone Oksana's age has been so successful.

OKSANA BAIUL
Born: November 16, 1977
Residence: Simsbury, Connecticut
Coach: Galina Zmievskaya
Choreographer: Eugeniy Nemirovsky

1993:	**2nd in European Championships**
	1st in World Championships
1994:	**2nd in European Championships**
	1st in Winter Olympics

Nicole Bobek

Among the top female skaters in the world, one of the great mysteries is American Nicole Bobek. Sometimes she seems like the best skater in her country. Other times she seems like a skater who would have trouble making her national team. She has not been at all consistent in her career.

Blessed with enormous skill and elegance, Nicole hasn't always trained with as much concentration as her coaches think she should. As a result, she has had nine different coaches.

"I can go through every coach in the world," Nicole says with a laugh.

That's just the way she is. If today's figure skaters are similar to rock 'n' roll stars, perhaps no one fits the description better than Nicole.

She wears several pierced earrings, she used to wear rings on all her fingers, and she tends to say whatever is on her mind. But most of all, Nicole does her own thing.

"Nicole is a person who likes to have fun," says world champion Todd Eldredge, who trained with Nicole in 1994–95, her best season.

"I'm free-spirited—I'm open," Nicole adds. "I don't hide much."

Her talent has never been hidden. Nicole first came into the spotlight in 1989 when, at 11 years of age, she finished second at the U.S. Novice Championships. But she then had very unpredictable results, which each of her coaches blamed on her lack of dedication to practice.

All that changed in the 1994–95 season when Nicole was with coach Richard Callaghan in Bloomfield Hills, Michigan, near Detroit.

And the results followed. Nicole won her first U.S. title, and followed that with a bronze medal at the World Championships a few weeks later.

Nicole grew up in Chicago and began skating when she was three years old. Her family didn't have much money, but her mother somehow found enough for skating lessons. Her mother made her practice the "spiral" move on their living room floor. Like former Olympic silver medalist Nancy Kerrigan, Nicole's spiral is her trademark.

When she became a celebrity after her national championship, Nicole was able to use the fame to help with a special project. In her campaign called "Touching the Heart—Raising the Spirit," Nicole visits schools and hospitals in the United States, to share stories about her skating and to help those in need. It is a side of Nicole that not many people know about.

When she is finished skating, Nicole hopes to become a figure skating TV broadcaster and also a choreographer, but before that she has some other business to take care of. Nicole did not make the American team for Worlds in 1996 because an injured ankle forced her to pull out of the nationals after the short program. Also, just before nationals, Nicole had changed coaches again—to Barbara Roles Williams.

Nicole will likely battle Michelle Kwan for the U.S. title and world medals until the 1998 Olympics in Nagano, Japan. Michelle's coach, Frank Carroll, is one of Nicole's many ex-coaches.

"Never, ever count Nicole out," Frank says.

NICOLE BOBEK
Born: August 23, 1977
Residence: Las Vegas, Nevada
Coach: Barbara Roles Williams

1993: 16th in World Junior Championships
5th in Trophée Lalique
5th in U.S. Championships
2nd in AT&T Pro-Am
1994: 3rd in U.S. Championships
13th in Group Qualifier at Worlds
4th in Hershey's Kisses Pro-Am
7th in Goodwill Games
7th in Skate America
5th in Thrifty Car Rental International
1995: 1st in U.S. Championships
3rd in World Championships
4th in Hershey's Kisses International
3rd in Nations Cup
6th in Skate America

Brian Boitano

If the line that divides professional and amateur skating is ever completely wiped out, it will be because of Brian Boitano.

The 1988 Olympic champion first became famous in the "Battle of the Brians" competitions with Canada's Brian Orser. He rewrote skating history when, after nearly six years as a professional, he began pressuring the International Skating Union for the right to return to amateur ranks for the 1994 Olympics. The resulting "Boitano Rule" permitted pro skaters to return to amateur competition if they met certain criteria. Brian gave up about a million dollars, which he would have made skating professionally that winter, for the chance to compete at the Lillehammer Olympics.

"I have plenty of money and my life doesn't really revolve around money," he explains. "It's more important to me to be secure with myself and know that I did everything in skating that I could."

Brian was able to succeed in his amateur comeback because he had such high standards and training discipline. Most pros ease up on their most difficult jumps because they have to perform a show every night, usually in a different city. Brian, however, practiced the triple Axel, the King of Jumps, every day and became well known for the consistency with which he landed it in his touring shows, Skating 1 and Skating 2. As a result, his skill level remained spectacularly high. Unlike many pros, he was able to match the amateurs jump for jump.

When Brian returned to amateur ranks, he admitted to some nervousness. But despite a sore back and badly aching knees from years of landing jumps, he finished second in the 1994 U.S. national championships and then sixth in the Olympics he had helped open up to professionals. Afterward, he reflected on his career, which he plans to continue in both professional and amateur skating. "I've done a lot of neat things in this sport," he said. "I appreciate my life."

Since he enrolled in group lessons in Sunnyvale, California, more than 22 years ago, Brian has had only one coach, Linda Leaver. Linda coached only one or two students at a time in order to give each of them more attention.

"Brian was the kind of kid who wouldn't get off the ice until the Zamboni ran him over," Linda laughs.

"I was a daredevil," Brian recalls. "The more dangerous the jump or spin, the more fun it was. I wanted to do something that no one else could do."

And he did. He won a cherished Olympic gold medal. He kept his sport in the public eye in the United States. And he made the line between professional and amateur skating so thin that it became almost invisible.

BRIAN BOITANO
Born: October 22, 1963
Residence: Sunnyvale, California
Coach: Linda Leaver
Choreographer: Sandra Bezic

1986:	1st in World Championships
	1st in U.S. Nationals
	1st in Skate America
1987:	1st in U.S. Nationals
	2nd in World Championships
	2nd in Skate Canada
	1st in Novarat Trophy
1988:	1st in U.S. Nationals
	1st in Winter Olympics
	1st in World Championships
1989:	1st in World Professional Championships
1990:	1st in World Professional Championships
1991:	1st in World Professional Championships
1992:	1st in World Professional Championships
1993:	1st in World Professional Championships
	1st in Hershey's Kisses Pro-Am
	1st in AT&T Pro-Am Challenge
	2nd in Skate America
1994:	2nd in U.S. Nationals
	6th in Winter Olympics

Shae-Lynn Bourne and Victor Kraatz

It was just an ordinary ice dance practice, but an extraordinary event took place.

After a training session at the 1994 Winter Olympics, all the dancers from the other countries had left the ice. But Shae-Lynn Bourne and Victor Kraatz stayed behind to work on the new style of skating that will eventually make them famous.

The Canadians glided around the rink, bent lower to the ice than seemed physically possible. They crouched like cats waiting to pounce. The audience stopped heading for the exits and headed back to their seats. They had never seen anything like this.

It takes a long time to rise to the top in this event, but Shae-Lynn and Victor have already made a name for themselves with their modern, slinky style.

By 1996, they had moved onto the podium at the World Championships, finishing third. It was Canada's only medal at the Worlds in Edmonton. It was also the first ice dancing medal for Canada since

1988, the year Tracy Wilson and Rob McCall retired.

Shae-Lynn and Victor were matched as partners because they have the same kind of "line" and action in their knees and legs.

"I kept calling up coaches and asking if they had anyone I could be a partner with," Victor recalls of his search in 1991. "I went to Montreal, but didn't find anyone there and was just about to leave."

But Claude Beaudoin, the manager of the Boucherville Arena, and coach Josée Picard suggested Victor spend a few minutes with a 16-year-old former pairs skater from Chatham, Ontario.

"Five minutes later we decided to try it for one week," Victor says. "Best decision I ever made."

Shae-Lynn is athletic and graceful, and her pairs skating has helped: "It brought some new ideas and a different approach to the dance partnership," she says. "I think one thing we're trying to show is that ice dancing is a sport, that there is a risk to it."

She and Victor and Uschi Keszler, their former choreographer, accidentally discovered a new way of training. They found that, by pushing a traffic cone along beside them with one hand, they could lean over much farther than normally while skating. Canadian Elvis Stojko dubbed the new idea "hydro-blading" and the name stuck. It brought a whole new look to figure skating, including ice dancing.

Shae-Lynn and Victor moved out of Montreal for the 1994–95 season and trained with former world champions Marina Klimova and Sergei Ponomarenko in California. They switched coaches again the following season and split their time between Uschi Keszler's rink near Philadelphia and Natalia Dubova's training center in Lake Placid, New York. After winning their bronze medal at Worlds, they made Natalia their only coach.

No Canadian ice dancers have ever won Olympic gold. For years, the Russians have almost "owned" the sport. But Shae-Lynn and Victor are hoping that will all change at the Winter Olympics in 1998.

Shae-Lynn Bourne
Born: January 24, 1976
Victor Kraatz
Born: April 7, 1971
Residence: Lake Placid, New York
Coach: Natalia Dubova

1992:	**1st in Grand Prix International**
	1st in Nebelhorn Trophy
	6th in Skate Canada
	1st in Canadian Junior Championships
1993:	**1st in Canadian Championships**
	14th in World Championships
	3rd in Skate Canada
	5th in Nations Cup
1994:	**1st in Canadian Championships**
	10th in Winter Olympics
	6th in World Championships
	1st in Skate Canada
1995:	**1st in Canadian Championships**
	4th in World Championships
	1st in Skate Canada
	2nd in NHK Trophy
1996:	**1st in Canadian Championships**
	4th in Champions Series Final
	3rd in World Championships

Isabelle Brasseur and Lloyd Eisler

If there is a lesson to be learned from the career of Canadian pairs team Isabelle Brasseur and Lloyd Eisler it is this: patience pays off.

"That's very true, in both our cases," says Lloyd. "They said I was the guy who was too old. I was already out of skating. I wouldn't last. I had had too many partners. Everyone thought Isabelle was too small, not strong enough, and couldn't jump.

"Nobody thought we'd stay together a year, let alone ten years."

They're still together and they've won a world championship, two world silver medals, and two Olympic bronze medals. They rank as one of the top pairs in Canadian history.

Lloyd had already retired and had started a career as a skating official when coaches Josée Picard and Eric Gillies asked him to come to Montreal to look at a possible pairs partner. She was seven years younger than Lloyd, and about a foot (30 cm) shorter. After a brief trial, Lloyd and Isabelle decided to skate together to see how it worked out. The two quickly became known for their huge throws and lifts, and for their triple lateral twist, the only one in the world.

In 1993 at Prague, they became only the second Canadian pair in 31 years to win the world championship. As the music ended and the couple knew they'd skated well enough to win, a sobbing Lloyd whispered to Isabelle, "This is for your dad." Isabelle's father, Gill, had died a few months earlier.

The Canadians' bronze at the 1994 Olympics was the highest finish of those who had never been professionals.

Isabelle had cracked a rib in training before the Olympics. She skated in pain throughout their medal performance. "I'll take four-and-a-half minutes of pain for an Olympic medal, though," she says.

Lloyd, Isabelle and Brian Orser are the only three Canadian skaters to win two Olympic medals. After their second Olympics, Lloyd and Isabelle turned professional, and have become one of the most popular pairs, if not *the* most popular, on the pro circuit. They are one of the funniest pairs teams in the world and have one routine where Lloyd dresses as the woman and Isabelle dresses as the man. She even picks him up and throws him!

Some of the best competitions in skating history were the battles in pro competitions between the veteran Canadian pair and Olympic champions Ekaterina Gordeeva and the late Sergei Grinkov.

Isabelle and Lloyd like to use nicknames: everyone knows him as "Herbie" and he calls her "Fred." They spent a couple of years as boyfriend-girlfriend. But they decided that their off-ice relationship might be hurting their chances at skating success. So they stopped going out together, but remain each other's best friend.

"I would do anything for her," explains Lloyd. "And I know that she would do anything for me."

Isabelle Brasseur
Born: July 28, 1970
Lloyd Eisler
Born: April 28, 1963
Residence: Montreal, Quebec
Coaches: Josée Picard, Eric Gillies
Choreographer: Julie Marcotte

1989:	**1st in Canadian Championships**
	7th in World Championships
	1st in Skate Electric
	2nd in Trophée Lalique
1990:	**3rd in Canadian Championships**
	2nd in World Championships
	1st in Skate Canada
	2nd in NHK Trophy
1991:	**1st in Canadian Championships**
	2nd in World Championships
	1st in Nations Cup
1992:	**1st in Canadian Championships**
	3rd in Winter Olympics
	3rd in World Championships
	4th in NHK Trophy
1993:	**1st in Canadian Championships**
	1st in World Championships
	2nd in Piruetten
	1st in NHK Trophy
1994:	**1st in Canadian Championships**
	3rd in Winter Olympics
	2nd in World Championships

Philippe Candeloro

When 22-year-old Philippe Candeloro stood on the medals podium at the 1994 Winter Olympics in Lillehammer, it was a major breakthrough for his country.

It had been 22 years since France had won a men's figure skating medal at the Olympic Games. Also, Philippe's bronze was just the fourth medal his country had ever won in the event.

"It will help our country, having this medal," Philippe says. "It will make more young children want to skate and win, and know that we can do it."

There are a lot of similarities between Philippe and Canadian world champion Elvis Stojko. Both advanced much more quickly in the jumps than in the artistic side of skating, but rounded out their styles in their early 20s. And both have had ankle injuries that hampered them at recent World Championships.

And both of them love motorcycles.

It was his motorcycle that may have caused Philippe to miss his first opportunity to skate in a Winter Olympics. He had a motorcycle accident and broke his foot. This forced him to miss a month of training.

Angry and disappointed that he had been left off the team for the 1992 Olympics at Albertville, Philippe turned in some of the best performances of his career over the following two years. "It hurt that I couldn't skate in the Olympics in my own country," he says. "But maybe that made me skate harder."

In 1994, he leapt over veterans Brian Boitano, Viktor Petrenko, and Kurt Browning to bag his bronze at the Olympics. A few months later he won the silver medal behind Elvis's gold at the World Championships. The next year, Philippe won the bronze at Worlds. But in 1996, he injured his ankle and performed poorly in the short program at Worlds. He skated well in the freeskate and rose to ninth overall, well below what the French fans had hoped for.

Philippe was the first skater ever to use the same theme for his short program as his freeskate. In honor of his father, who was born in Italy, he skated to music from the *Godfather* movies in both programs.

"It's a new style of choreography," Philippe says. "Until I was 15, I hated choreography. I was worried that my friends, who are all hockey players, would tease me. But then I started to feel the choreography and understand it."

Philippe was seven-and-a-half when he first started skating, once a week with his school class. He wanted hockey skates, but only figure skates were available. After two weeks, André Brunet, who still coaches him, suggested to his parents that he begin private lessons because his natural ability was obvious.

He would spend six hours on the ice and then take school classes with other athletes right at the arena in Colombes. Now the arena is part of the National Training Center for skaters and other athletes at Colombes.

"It's good, because skaters are normal people, we are not rich," Philippe says. "Before, it was too expensive to come and skate, so kids did other things. With a training center, they stay skating."

PHILIPPE CANDELORO
Born: February 17, 1972
Residence: Colombes, France
Coach: André Brunet
Choreographer: Natacha Daddabie

1990:	8th in European Championships
	14th in World Championships
1991:	5th in European Championships
1992:	9th in World Championships
	1st in NHK Trophy
1993:	2nd in European Championships
	5th in World Championships
	2nd in Piruetten
	2nd in Trophée Lalique
	1st in NHK Trophy
1994:	5th in European Championships
	3rd in Winter Olympics
	2nd in World Championships
1995:	4th in European Championships
	3rd in World Championships
	3rd in NHK Trophy
1996:	5th in St. Petersburg Centennial
	5th in European Championships
	9th in World Championships

Lu Chen

Lu Chen stood smiling on the Olympic podium. She waved to the millions of people celebrating back home. China had won its first Olympic figure skating medal.

The slim but powerful Lu was just 17 when she captured the Olympic bronze in 1994. She is expected to be on the world scene for a long time to come. And other Chinese skaters are expected to follow, as Lu's successes make the sport more popular in her homeland. Although China had no indoor rinks just a few years ago, six were under construction after Lu won her first medal.

And skating in China has become even more popular since Lu won her country's first world championship in 1995. Lu, whose nickname is "Lulu," finished second to Michelle Kwan in the 1996 Worlds. It was one of the most exciting women's freeskates ever, and Lu received two perfect 6.0 marks for her brilliant performance. Three of the nine judges felt Lu had won, and the other six voted for Michelle. But either of them could have been world champion on that night. The two are expected to battle for gold medals all the way to the 1998 Olympics.

Lu first attracted attention in 1990 when, at the age of 14, she finished third at the World Junior Championships in Budapest.

"She just suddenly appeared, out of nowhere," recalls Sally Rehorick, a veteran Canadian judge and team leader. "There's a finish and a polish to her skating for someone so young. She always has programs that use the ice in a surprising way, with unusual angles and ways of approaching jumps."

In late 1976, when Lu was born, China's leaders were not interested in international sports, particularly figure skating. Although there were outdoor rinks in northern China, there was not one indoor rink in the entire country. There was no experienced coaching. But Lu came from a very athletic family. Her father was an ice hockey player. Her mother excelled at table tennis, a big sport in China. Lu got her first skates soon after she could walk. It didn't take her long, her father recalls, before "she could glide with ease. It was amazing how the little girl took to the ice."

Lu was just five years old when she entered an amateur sports school in Jilin Province in northeast China. There she hooked up with coach Li Ming Zhu. Li knew right away that she had someone special on her hands. "When she was just nine years old, she did a triple jump," her coach says. "At that time, no one in China could make a triple jump."

In 1992, Lu gave China its first figure skating medal ever, a bronze at the World Championships in Oakland. She followed that up with a bronze the next year, and her historic bronze at the 1994 Olympics.

Lu spent time before the Olympics training at Lake Arrowhead, California. While there, she was the special guest of the Ice Castle Training Center.

Sometimes she thinks back to being nine years old, trying to become the first Chinese skater to do a triple jump. "I was very proud and willing to try," she says. "When everyone thought no one could do it, I felt I could do it."

LU CHEN
Born: November 24, 1976
Residence: Chang Chun, China
Coach: Li Ming Zhu
Choreographer: Sandra Bezic

1990:	3rd in World Junior Championships
1991:	3rd in World Junior Championships
1992:	6th in Winter Olympics
	3rd in World Championships
	3rd in Skate America
1993:	3rd in World Championships
	3rd in Piruetten
	3rd in NHK Trophy
	1st in Skate Canada
1994:	3rd in Winter Olympics
1995:	1st in World Championships
	2nd in Skate America
	2nd in Trophée de France
	1st in NHK Trophy
1996:	4th in Champions Series Final
	2nd in World Championships

Todd Eldredge

By the time he was 19 years old, Todd Eldredge had won two U.S. championships and a bronze medal at the World Championships.

Then, for the next four years, the figure skating world seemed to forget about him.

But there's no forgetting about Todd Eldredge now, not after he won the 1995 American title and the 1996 World Championships.

Todd gave the U.S. its first men's title since 1988 when he won Worlds at Edmonton on a night many called the greatest ever in men's skating. But with Elvis Stojko, Philippe Candeloro, Ilya Kulik, Rudy Galindo and Sebastien Britten all skating superbly, it was Todd who was the best.

TODD ELDREDGE
Born: August 28, 1971
Residence: Bloomfield Hills, Michigan
Coaches: Richard Callaghan, Kirk Wyse
Choreographers: Richard Callaghan, Kirk Wyse

1991:	**1st in U.S. Championships**
	3rd in World Championships
	1st in U.S. Olympic Festival
	3rd in Skate America
1992:	**7th in World Championships**
	10th in Winter Olympics
	1st in Nations Cup
	1st in Skate America
1993:	**6th in U.S. Championships**
	4th in AT&T Pro-Am
	1st in Trophée Lalique
	4th in Skate America
1994:	**4th in U.S. Championships**
	2nd in Hershey's Kisses Pro-Am
	2nd in Goodwill Games
	1st in Skate America
	1st in Thrifty Car Rental International
	1st in NHK Trophy
1995:	**1st in U.S. Championships**
	2nd in World Championships
	1st in Hershey's Kisses International
	1st in Skate America
	3rd in Nations Cup
	3rd in Starlight Challenge
1996:	**2nd in U.S. Championships**
	5th in Champions Series Final
	1st in World Championships

"Once my nerves started relaxing a bit, I really got into the program," Todd said. "It was probably one of the best performances I've ever had, if not *the* best."

It had been an inconsistent season for Todd, after he returned to the upper level of skating the year before. "I think it all came a little too early for me," he says now. In 1991, he won his second American title and a bronze medal at Worlds, but then began a very difficult three-year period in his skating career.

He had back troubles the following year and could not skate at nationals.

The next year, he felt that judges and other skating officials didn't like his skating style. He admits now that he lost much of his enthusiasm for training that season and did not come close to making the U.S. team. A year later, in 1994, he missed the team again.

That's when people began to forget about Todd. But he was determined to make them remember. He won three straight fall internationals in 1994, won the U.S. championship again, and took a silver medal at Worlds, narrowly losing out to Elvis Stojko.

"If I think back on all the things that happened during those years—the back injury, the real bad year in 1993, missing the 1994 Olympic team—yeah, it seems like I've been around forever." Todd smiles. "But I think with those years I wasn't really around. It made skating all newer to me, a bit fresher."

Eldredge became the first man in American skating history to win back his national championship after three years of not winning a medal of any kind. It was quite a comeback, which was completed March 21, 1996, at the Edmonton Coliseum when he won the title over Ilya Kulik. Todd landed two triple-triple combinations, while Ilya landed only one, and that was the difference.

"In 1995 [when Todd was second], the skating in the men's final was so good that I didn't think it could ever be better," said Todd's coach, Richard Callaghan.

"I was wrong. This was better."

Rudy Galindo

People used to wonder why Rudy Galindo kept on skating. They don't wonder anymore.

Until the 1996 national championships, Rudy was overlooked on the American skating scene. At one time, he had realistic hopes of winning a medal at a world championship, but as a pairs skater. He and his partner, Kristi Yamaguchi, won the U.S. championships in 1989 and 1990 and finished fifth in the world both years. But along with her pairs skating, Kristi wanted to concentrate on her singles career. So their partnership dissolved in 1990.

It turned out to be a good decision for Kristi, because she won two world championships and the 1992 Olympic gold medal. But it left Rudy out in the cold. "It was sad times," Rudy recalls. "Then it turned to anger, but I got over that pretty quickly. I can see now that if I were her, I would have done the same thing. I decided to concentrate on singles. I thought if I could hang on to get on as the third-place guy at nationals, I could get to Worlds. It just took me a while."

When Rudy did finally get to Worlds it was not as "the third-place guy at nationals" but as American champion. Because he had finished eighth the year before—and had never been higher than fifth— nobody gave him much of a chance before the 1996 U.S. Championships in his home town of San Jose. But he skated beautifully to win the title, capturing two perfect 6.0s in the freeskate. Many in the capacity crowd felt it was the greatest performance they had ever seen, as he landed eight triples and lyrically interpreted the music from *Swan Lake*. It was the most talked about figure skating story of the year.

But there was more to come.

Rudy sprained his left ankle—twice—after nationals. The second time he was forced to withdraw from an important international event in Russia, just three weeks before the World Championships. But he overcame the injury to win the bronze medal at the Worlds in Edmonton, where he had once trained with Kristi.

"It was great to know that nationals wasn't just a once-in-a-lifetime performance," Rudy said.

For Rudy, the road to fame and fortune was long and bumpy. Skating is a very expensive sport and Rudy didn't have much money. He lived in a trailer park with his mother. To cut down on expenses, he rode his bicycle to the rink to train. His sister Laura was also his coach and didn't charge him for lessons, "and sometimes she lent me money." And he was saddened by the deaths of his father, his older brother and two of his former coaches, all within a short period of time.

But he refused to give up, and stuck at his skating. All the hard work and dedication paid off. After seven years of trying, he won his U.S. championship at the age of 26. He was the second oldest men's champion in American history. The oldest was 51-year-old Chris Christenson, who won in 1926.

Then, less than two months later, he and world champion Todd Eldredge gave the United States its best men's finish at Worlds in 15 years. During Worlds he got an important phone call from his former partner. "Kristi said she watched me on TV and told me to stay focused," Rudy remembers. "She said she's so proud of me."

A lot of people were very proud of Rudy.

RUDY GALINDO
Born: September 7, 1969
Residence: San Jose, California
Coach: Laura Galindo
Choreographer: John Brancotto

1990:	**5th in World Championships (in pairs with Kristi Yamaguchi)**
1992:	**2nd in Prague Skate**
1993:	**5th in U.S. Championships**
	2nd in U.S. Olympic Festival
	4th in Nations Cup
1994:	**7th in U.S. Championships**
	1st in Karl Schäfer Memorial
1995:	**8th in U.S. Championships**
1996:	**1st in U.S. Championships**
	3rd in World Championships

Ekaterina Gordeeva and Sergei Grinkov

"G & G" means only one thing in figure skating circles: Ekaterina Gordeeva and Sergei Grinkov, the incredible pairs champions of not one, but two Olympics.

People called them the greatest pairs team of all time, a perfect couple who had nothing but a bright future to look forward to. But in Lake Placid, New York, during a practice session for the Stars on Ice tour on Monday, November 20, 1995, Sergei Grinkov suddenly collapsed and died. He and Ekaterina (or Katia, as she likes to be called) had just finished a move when he fell to the ice, cradled by his wife.

The news devastated the entire figure skating world. Sergei and Katia were very popular with audiences, and fans wondered if she would go on. In February 1996, she answered them by skating alone at a special Stars on Ice tribute to her husband in Hartford, Connecticut. It was a beautiful and haunting program. With a return to performing helping her overcome the death, she skated solo on the Canadian and Asian tours of Stars on Ice and agreed to do the same for the 1996-97 American tour.

Meanwhile, the memory of G & G's brilliant career lives on. In 1986, they won their first senior world championship in Geneva, Switzerland, when Katia was just 16. They impressed the judges with their side-by-side jumps and the power of their pairs tricks.

Like many duos, when they first began skating together G & G were known as a "Mutt and Jeff" team. In skating, this means the man is much bigger than the woman. He is able to lift her high above his head and throw her long distances. Over time, Katia grew but the pair's throws remained big and strong.

After winning four world titles and the 1988 Olympic gold in Calgary, Katia and Sergei became professionals in late 1990. They performed in professional skating shows, such as Stars on Ice.

When the International Skating Union decided to allow professionals to compete in the Olympics, Katia and Sergei talked it over. They decided to take a year off touring. In their amateur comeback, they won the Russian, European, and Olympic championships.

"The years on tour helped our skating be more professional, more polished," said Katia. "It made us much better partners than we were before."

That was true both on and off the ice. In April 1991, Katia and Sergei were married. A year and a half later, they had a daughter, Daria. They were a truly international family, with homes in both Moscow and Tampa, Florida.

Katia has written a book, with Ed Swift of *Sports Illustrated*, called *My Sergei*. It talks of their life and career together.

In an emotional speech after her return to the ice in 1996, she told the audience: "Try to find happiness in every day at least once. Smile at each other every day and say to each other just one extra time, 'I love you.'"

Ekaterina Gordeeva
Born: May 28, 1971
Sergei Grinkov
Born: February 4, 1967
Died: November 20, 1995
Residence: Tampa/Moscow
Coach: Vladimir Zaharov
Choreographer: Marina Zueva

1986: 1st in World Championships
2nd in European Championships
1987: 1st in World Championships
1st in European Championships
1988: 1st in Winter Olympics
1st in European Championships
2nd in World Championships
1989: 1st in World Championships
1990: 1st in Goodwill Games
1st in European Championships
1st in World Championships
1991: 1st in World Challenge of Champions (pro)
1st in World Professional Championships
1992: 1st in World Professional Championships
1993: 1st in Skate Canada
1994: 1st in European Championships
1st in Winter Olympics
1st in Canadian Pro Championships
1st in North American Pro Championships
1st in World Team Championships
1st in World Pro Championships
1995: 1st in World Challenge

Nancy Kerrigan

There is almost no one, anywhere, who has not heard about the incredible events that took place in Nancy Kerrigan's life in early 1994.

She had improved her skating dramatically over a disappointing 1993 season. However, she suffered serious knee injuries when a man attacked her during a practice session at the American championships. Nancy was forced to withdraw from the competition. At first she wasn't sure if she would skate again. Yet through enormous effort — swimming, weightlifting, and riding an exercise bike — Nancy recovered in time to win the silver medal seven weeks later at the Winter Olympics in Lillehammer, Norway.

"Nancy Kerrigan can do everything in this sport," praises Canadian champion Josée Chouinard.

Josée was among many skaters who thought Nancy skated well enough to win the 1994 Olympic gold. As it was, she lost to Oksana Baiul by the smallest margin possible: one mark on one judge's card.

The silver medal was still a triumph over high odds, however. With her bronze medal from the 1992 Games, Nancy became only the fourth American woman, and first since 1960, to win medals in two Olympics.

A strong jumper who has mastered everything up to and including the very difficult triple Lutz, Nancy excels at other technical elements that make up freeskating. She has a strong skating stroke, marvelous spins, and impressive footwork.

But it is what Nancy does with those technical skills that sets her apart from most skaters. She has an artistic flair and an ability to interpret music that make her lyrical and elegant on the ice. Nancy also has one of the most famous faces in North America. She was on the 1992 year-end cover of *Life* magazine. *People* magazine selected her as one of the 50 most beautiful people in America.

Nancy came into her Olympic year training more seriously than at any point in her career. She worked out with the videotape "Abs of Steel" to get stronger. She had sessions with a psychologist to help her mental preparation.

Like many skating families, the Kerrigans (she has two older brothers) are no strangers to hard work and sacrifice. Nancy's father, Dan, put in overtime at his job to help pay for her lessons. Her mother, Brenda, is legally blind. One of Nancy's major off-ice projects is working with the International Lions Club's Sight First program. It helps in finding cures for blindness.

This hard-working and courageous skater's comeback from the attack to almost winning Olympic gold won her millions of new fans.

"I was really proud of myself," she said after receiving her silver medal. "And to watch the American flag be raised after what I put in just to be here, it was thrilling."

It was thrilling for everybody.

NANCY KERRIGAN
Born: October 13, 1969
Residence: Stoneham, Massachusetts
Coaches: Mary and Evy Scotvold
Choreographers: Mary Scotvold, Mark Militano

1990:	4th in U.S. Nationals
	3rd in Skate Electric
	1st in U.S. Olympic Festival
	4th in Goodwill Games
	3rd in Trophée Lalique
1991:	3rd in U.S. Nationals
	3rd in World Championships
	3rd in Trophée Lalique
	1st in Nations Cup
1992:	2nd in U.S. Nationals
	3rd in Winter Olympics
	2nd in World Championships
	2nd in Skate America
	1st in Chrysler Pro-Am
1993:	1st in U.S. Nationals
	5th in World Championships
	2nd in Hershey's Kisses Pro-Am
	1st in Piruetten
	1st in AT&T Pro-Am
1994:	2nd in Winter Olympics

Michelle Kwan

When the scoreboard at the Edmonton Coliseum flashed up the standings, Michelle Kwan could not believe it.

"I thought, 'I'm the world champion.' Oh, my God. I've dreamed about that since I was little."

That was not so very long ago. When Michelle won the World Championships in a fantastic showdown with 1995 champion Lu Chen in Edmonton in March of 1996, it was still four months until her sixteenth birthday. That made her the third youngest women's champion of all time, behind Sonja Henie and Oksana Baiul.

Many say that the women's freeskate final of the 1996 Worlds was the best in 20 years, if not in modern times. Lu skated and got two perfect 6.0s, and soon it was Michelle's turn.

"After I heard Lulu's marks I thought I'd have to do a quadruple jump to win," Michelle said. No women skater does a quadruple in competition, but Michelle did land seven triple jumps. On the last one, she turned a planned double Axel into a triple

because she felt she needed one more than Lu's six triples, and when she finished the crowd jumped to their feet and started yelling, "Six. Six. Six," just as they did after Lu skated. Then the marks came up and Michelle also had two perfect 6.0s. She was the new champion.

"I've never seen two performances like that in my life," said Morry Stillwell, president of the United States Figure Skating Association.

Nobody has. And very few people have ever had a skating career that has gone so far in such a short time as Michelle's.

At an early age, she was recognized as having great skill, but she was inconsistent, and placed only ninth at the U.S. Junior Championships in 1992.

The next year, when she was just 12, the youngest skater at the U.S. senior nationals in 19 years, she finished an encouraging sixth. The following year, when Nancy Kerrigan was injured by an attacker and missed the competition, she was second and got to go to the Olympics as an alternate in case either Nancy or Tonya Harding could not compete. Both did, but Michelle took part in the Worlds and finished eighth.

She was fourth in the 1995 World Championships with a performance that one magazine poll voted the best of the whole season. Her coach thought she might have won a medal had she been a bit older and appeared more polished on the ice. So the next season she came back looking more mature, and she skated the very sophisticated *Salome* program. After winning three fall internationals in the Champions Series (Skate Canada, Skate America and Nations Cup), Michelle became its first grand champion when she won the Champions Series Final in Paris.

Each of her victories in the 1996 season brought Michelle a lot of prize money ($200,000 in all), but it was the world title that mattered most.

"It was the World Championships and I skated the very best of my life," she said. "Then the emotions just took over."

MICHELLE KWAN
Born: July 7, 1980
Residence: Los Angeles, California
Coach: Frank Carroll
Choreographer: Lori Nichol

1994:	**1st in Junior World Championships**
	2nd in U.S. Championships
	8th in World Championships
	2nd in Hershey's Kisses Pro-Am
	2nd in Skate America
	2nd in Goodwill Games
	3rd in Trophée de France
1995:	**2nd in U.S. Championships**
	4th in World Championships
	1st in Hershey's Kisses International
	1st in Skate America
	1st in Skate Canada
	1st in Nations Cup
1996:	**1st in U.S. Championships**
	3rd in St. Petersburg Centennial
	1st in Champions Series Final
	1st in World Championships

Jenni Meno and Todd Sand

When Jenni Meno and Todd Sand take to the ice, you can see the romance and the passion in their skating. That's not surprising. If they made a movie of their career, it would be called *Love Story*.

A few years ago, Jenni and Todd were good friends but were skating with other pairs partners. Jenni skated with Scott Wendland and Todd's partner was Natasha Kuchiki. They all trained together with coach John Nicks in Costa Mesa, California.

Both pairs qualified for the 1992 Olympics in Albertville. After their event was over, Jenni and Todd spent a lot of time together. They realized they were attracted to each other and wanted to skate together.

"We found out we had the same goals, including a desire to skate to classical music," Todd said. "A lot of American pairs are just thrown together and coached in a certain way. We had a really solid idea of how we wanted to skate and where we wanted to go."

After the 1992 Worlds, they formed their partner-ship and have been together ever since—on and off the ice. There must be something romantic about the Olympics, because they started their relationship at the 1992 games, and at the 1994 games in Lillehammer they became engaged. In the summer of 1995 they were married.

"I see an extraordinary closeness between them," says their coach, John Nicks. The chemistry between them is obvious. At the 1995 U.S. Championships, they received six perfect 6.0 scores for artistic impression, an extremely rare set of marks in pairs skating. In 1996, they won their third straight national title.

After finishing fifth and sixth in the World Championships, they won the bronze medal at Worlds in 1995. But they had to rise from fifth place after the short program with a strong freeskate. The same thing happened the next year. Jenni and Todd did not skate well in the short program at Worlds and were again ranked fifth. Todd was very angry about their performance, but the couple used that emotion positively to help them skate superbly in the freeskate.

"I was excited with the way we skated last year," said Todd after their second bronze. "This year, I'm very *proud* of the way we skated."

With their international successes, Meno and Sand have given the United States a new life in pairs skating. Only two American couples have ever won the World Championships in pairs. Since Tai Babilonia and Randy Gardner won Worlds in 1979, Americans have won only five medals in pairs. Jenni and Todd have two of those, and Todd had another when he and Natasha won the bronze in 1991.

No American pairs team has ever won an Olympic gold medal, and they are hoping they'll become the first, in 1998 at Nagano. They have increased their skating speed by hard practice, and continue to improve other technical elements.

"Because of our relationship, it's easier for us," Jenni says. "When we go out to compete, we know how much we care about each other and we try to show everyone just how much we love to skate together."

Jenni Meno
Born: November 19, 1970
Todd Sand
Born: October 30, 1963
Residence: Costa Mesa, California
Coach: John Nicks
Choreographer: John Nicks

1992:	**1st in Prague Skate**
1993:	**2nd in U.S. Championships**
	5th in World Championships
	1st in AT&T Pro-Am
	3rd in Trophée Lalique
1994:	**1st in U.S. Championships**
	5th in Winter Olympics
	6th in World Championships
	1st in Hershey's Kisses Pro-Am
	2nd in Thrifty Car Rental International
	5th in NHK Trophy
1995:	**1st in U.S. Championships**
	3rd in World Championships
	2nd in Skate America
	3rd in Trophée de France
1996:	**1st in U.S. Championships**
	4th in Champions Series Final
	3rd in World Championships

Elvis Stojko

Yes, he is named after *that* Elvis. Irene and Steve Stojko were Elvis Presley fans. Even before their first son was born in 1972, they had decided to name him after their musical hero. So it seemed almost destined that Elvis Stojko should hit the world stage.

For many years, though, despite a reputation as one of the best skaters in the world, Elvis could not escape the shadow of another Canadian skater. That's understandable, since the huge shadow was cast by Kurt Browning, the most accomplished men's skater his country had ever produced.

Like many of the great Canadian men before him, Elvis was loudly praised for his jumping strength and foot speed. In just his second world championship

ELVIS STOJKO
Born: March 22, 1972
Residence: Richmond Hill, Ontario
Coaches: Doug and Michelle Leigh
Choreographer: Uschi Keszler

1990: **2nd in Canadian Championships**
　　　　3rd in Trophée Lalique
　　　　8th in Skate America
　　　　9th in World Championships
1991: **2nd in Canadian Championships**
　　　　6th in World Championships
　　　　1st in Skate Canada
1992: **2nd in Canadian Championships**
　　　　7th in Winter Olympics
　　　　2nd in NHK Trophy
　　　　1st in Skate Canada
　　　　3rd in World Championships
1993: **2nd in Canadian Championships**
　　　　2nd in World Championships
　　　　1st in Piruetten
1994: **1st in Canadian Championships**
　　　　2nd in Winter Olympics
　　　　1st in World Championships
　　　　1st in Nations Cup
　　　　1st in Skate Canada
1995: **1st in World Championships**
　　　　3rd in Trophée de France
　　　　1st in NHK Trophy
1996: **1st in Canadian Championships**
　　　　2nd in Champions Series Final
　　　　4th in World Championships

appearance, at the age of 18, he entered the record book as the first skater ever to use a quadruple jump in combination with another jump. At competitions, his consistency in landing all the toughest jumps earned him the nickname "The Terminator." But he was criticized for his lack of artistry.

During a frigid week in early 1994 in the northern Canadian city of Edmonton, Elvis finally skated out of Kurt Browning's shadow and into his own spotlight. He won his first Canadian championship. Then a month later he won the silver medal at the Winter Olympics. Many people watching felt he should have been awarded the gold.

Those fans didn't have to wait long. Less than a month later, at the World Championships in Japan, Elvis skated brilliantly and became the fifth Canadian man to win the world championship.

Although skating is his first love, Elvis is intensely interested in several other pursuits. He is known for his interest in dirt-bike racing and martial arts such as karate and kung fu.

Elvis won the Worlds again in 1995, but it was not easy. He badly injured his ankle and had to withdraw from the Canadian Championships. It appeared he would not be able to skate at Worlds, but despite a very, very sore ankle, he decided to take part. In the freeskate, he changed a planned triple-double at the end of his program into a triple-triple, and that was enough to beat American Todd Eldredge, who also skated superbly. This victory was very satisfying because an injured ankle would have kept many skaters on the sidelines. "You are Superman," his coach, Doug Leigh, said when Elvis came off the ice.

In 1996, Elvis had a rare fall on his triple Axel in the short program and was out of the running for the medals. But he was magnificent in the long program. He earned a lengthy standing ovation and rose to fourth place overall. The likable Canadian champion should be back in the medals for 1997.

Jayne Torvill and Christopher Dean

Jayne Torvill and Christopher Dean have been called the greatest ice dancers who ever lived and the biggest creative influence on skating's modern era. They are also the only dancers to win medals in Olympics held ten years apart.

Especially in their first turn as amateurs, when they won four World Championships and an Olympic gold in the early 1980s, Jayne and Chris were the "princess and prince" of the arena. Like royalty, they remained somewhat aloof and withdrawn from their adoring public. There was constant speculation as to whether they would get married. (They eventually did, although not to each other.)

And like a prince and princess, they were often treated differently than others. Ice dancing's rules were loosened to make room for their creative routines, which were unlike those of any other dancers' before them. They had many unforgettable programs. In one they portrayed various circus acts — jugglers, clowns, elephants — to the theme from the musical *Barnum*. In another, they imitated a bullfighter.

This royal couple reached the heights of skating fame despite some very unroyal beginnings. They were both born in the northern English town of Nottingham, best known for the legend of Robin Hood, not world-class skaters. There was only one small rink in the city. Because it was usually packed during regular skating times and because each of them had to work to support themselves, they trained at unusual, and tiring, hours. They'd often start practice at 10:30 p.m. and skate until 2:00 in the morning. Then they would try to grab another hour of training at 9:00 a.m. before heading off to their jobs. Jayne was a clerk for an insurance company. Chris was a police constable. One week, he missed three night practices because he was arresting criminals.

Eventually the city of Nottingham provided the promising couple with a cash grant to enable them to train fulltime without having to worry about outside employment. That's when they began their spectacular rise at the international level.

In 1982 they set a stunning record of 14 perfect 6.0 marks for their freeskate routine at the World Championships. They then raised their standards even higher, to 16 sixes the following year, including the only time in history all nine judges had ever given anyone 6.0 for artistic impression.

When they turned professional, Jayne and Chris went on to new levels of creativity before coming back to win the bronze medal at the 1994 Olympics.

"We got so many letters and postcards from supporters afterwards, who said they loved what we did, that that was like a gold medal to us," said Chris.

We don't see Torvill and Dean skate on tour in North America as often as we'd like to because they spend much of their time in Europe. Chris also choreographs programs for other world-class ice dancing couples, and he and Jayne design their own large shows and appear on television in England.

They're back to professional skating now. But Torvill and Dean left behind an amateur world that they changed forever—and for the better.

Jayne Torvill
Born: October 7, 1957
Christopher Dean
Born: July 27, 1958
Residence: Nottingham, England
Coaches: Betty Callaway, Bobby Thompson, Andris Toppe
Choreographers: Jayne Torvill, Christopher Dean

1980:	5th in Winter Olympics
	4th in World Championships
1981:	1st in World Championships
	1st in St. Ivel Championships
	1st in European Championships
1982:	1st in World Championships
	1st in European Championships
1983:	1st in World Championships
1984:	1st in Winter Olympics
	1st in World Championships
	1st in World Professional Championships
1985:	1st in World Professional Championships
1990:	1st in World Professional Championships
1994:	1st in European Championships
	3rd in Winter Olympics

Kristi Yamaguchi

Like so many American skaters her age, Kristi Yamaguchi was inspired as a young girl by the fame and success achieved by Dorothy Hamill, who won the 1976 Olympic gold medal.

When Kristi began taking lessons in Fremont, California, not even she would have predicted that she would become the first U.S. women's Olympic champion since Dorothy's famous victory at Innsbruck, Austria. In 1992 in Albertville, France, Kristi became just the fifth U.S. woman to win Olympic gold.

Kristi won a clear victory in Albertville over Japan's jumping sensation, Midori Ito, with an elegant, artistic performance that also included six perfectly landed triple jumps. "All of the articles in the newspapers before the 1992 Olympics were about the battle between artistry and athleticism," Kristi says. "I hope in some way I did show that [the two] can be combined."

All through her skating career, Kristi has been able to take ideas that seem like opposites and bring them together. She is slender and graceful. But she is also strong enough to land triple toe loops, triple flips, triple Salchows, and triple Lutzes consistently, night after night. And she is the only American female of

her generation to compete in two different events at the same World Championships. Until 1990 she and Rudy Galindo were the best pairs team in the U.S.

It was a very difficult lifestyle, trying to combine both singles and pairs skating at such a high level. Kristi was living in Edmonton, Alberta, because her singles coach, Christy Ness, had moved there. But she also had to fly back 1000 miles (1600 km) to Dublin, California, to practice pairs with Rudy and their pairs coach, Jim Hulick. After the 1990 World Championships, when she and Rudy were fifth and she was fourth in singles, Kristi decided she would have to give up pairs and concentrate on singles. It was a wise decision because the next year in Munich she won her first world championship at the age of 19. It took Rudy longer, but he won the men's singles title in 1996.

In a strange twist, Kristi won a world championship before she was even judged the best skater in her own country. In 1991, she was second to Tonya Harding at the U.S. Nationals. But Kristi won the world championship a month later, as American women (she, Tonya, and Nancy Kerrigan) swept the medals. Her only American title came in her fabulous 1992 season, when she was U.S., Olympic, and world champion.

After that brilliant end to her amateur career, Kristi turned professional with Stars on Ice. When professionals were allowed back into the Olympics, she thought long and hard before deciding not to return to amateur ranks. "I really looked into my heart and waited until the last possible minute before making the decision," she says. "But I finally realized that, in my amateur career, I had accomplished all — and more — than I set out to do."

As a headliner with Stars on Ice, Kristi is one of the world's most popular professional skaters. She's won several major professional championships, including the Gold Championships, which only Olympic gold medalists are permitted to enter. Many American skaters, including Michelle Kwan, have said that Kristi was an inspiration to them. Just as Dorothy Hamill was to a young Kristi Yamaguchi.

KRISTI YAMAGUCHI
Born: July 12, 1971
Residence: Freemont, California
Coach: Christy Ness

1988:	1st in World Junior Championships (women)
	1st in World Junior Championships (pairs)
1989:	2nd in U.S. Nationals
	6th in World Championships
1990:	2nd in U.S. Nationals
	4th in World Championships
1991:	2nd in U.S. Nationals
	1st in World Championships
1992:	1st in U.S. Nationals
	1st in Winter Olympics
	1st in World Championships
	1st Challenge of Champions (pro)
1993:	2nd in World Pro Championships
1994:	1st in Gold Championships
	1st in World Pro Championships
1995:	1st in Gold Championships

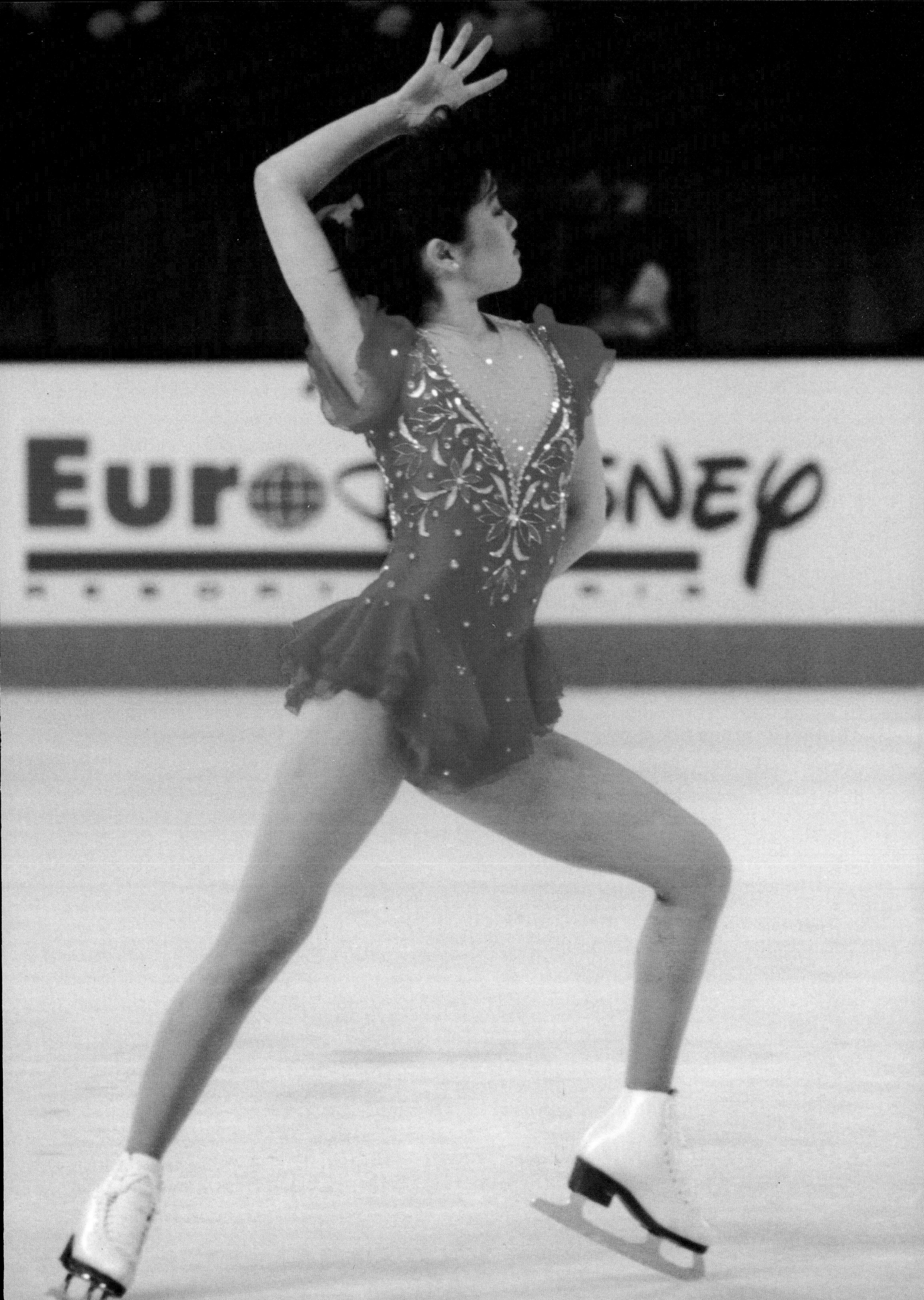

From Practice to the Podium

At the peak of the figure skating mountain, one season barely ends before the next one begins.

After the World Championships, there is an exhibition tour of the major cities on the continent on which the championships were held. The leading skaters perform show programs before huge audiences. In addition to the World Tour, show programs are used for other events that aren't competitions. These include guest appearances on TV and at carnivals, and pro tours.

Skaters love their show programs because there are fewer rules and no judges. The exhibitions can be skated to any kind of music. They are usually funnier or more dramatic than the competitive programs. Isabelle Brasseur and Lloyd Eisler, for instance, have a hilarious show routine in which their roles are reversed. She plays the man and he plays the woman. And Elvis Stojko came into his own as a performer with his wild rock 'n' roll show program to the pounding music of Eddie Van Halen.

The music: it must be right

Music plays a key role at every level of skating. Show programs and professional skaters' routines are accompanied by whatever music the performer wants to use. Amateur skaters in competition, on the other hand, are ruled by far stricter codes. The music must be all instrumental; no vocals are allowed. And it's essential for skaters to pick music that allows them to show off their best skills. Their music should also have some changes of speed and rhythm. In the ice dance, only certain rhythms may be used.

Sometime in early summer, once the world's best skaters have finished with the spring tour, they take two or three weeks' holiday. Then they go right back to training for the next year.

And they start by choosing the music. Nothing else can happen until then.

The skater, coach, and choreographer make this decision together, but the skater has the last word. After all, it is the skater who must perform to it in practice, day after day, month after month.

"You listen, and listen, and listen to music," explains Kathy Casey, coach of American champion Scott Davis. "You probably listen to 50 pieces. And that's after you've already narrowed it down to your general idea. Otherwise, you'd never find the right music."

Nancy Kerrigan loves Neil Diamond. She's from Boston, so she felt comfortable and relaxed skating to the Boston Pops' medley of Neil Diamond hits. Previously, she had chosen music with more definite themes: from the movies *Born on the Fourth of July* and *Beauty and the Beast*.

The trend today is for skaters to perform a theme piece — an idea piece. For example, at the 1994 Olympics, Kurt Browning portrayed 1940s movie star Humphrey Bogart. Philippe Candeloro was the Godfather. Elvis Stojko celebrated martial arts. The use of a theme had been made popular during the early 1980s by Torvill and Dean with their single-idea programs.

Sometimes the music a skater likes isn't precisely what the program requires. It might be a few bars too long in the footwork section. Or the loudest, most dramatic sounds might occur a few notes after they're needed for a big jump. So bits are taken out, or some might be repeated or added from another part of the piece to bring it all together. Kurt Browning chose the music from the movie *Casablanca* to match his Humphrey Bogart theme. However, the ending wasn't long enough. So the final few notes of music had to be stretched out. Some skaters join two completely different pieces of music together, so the program includes different rhythms. All this patching and changing is done in a recording studio and can cost a lot of money.

"Music is expensive, yes," says Kurt Browning. "It's worth it though because, when it's right, no one notices that one piece blends into the next. It's seamless."

Mapping out the program

Once the music is chosen, it is cut down to its proper length (2 minutes, 40 seconds for technical programs; 4 minutes for women's freeskate; 4 minutes, 30 seconds for men's). The elements must then be added to it. Most skaters have a choreographer to help them map out their program, to achieve the best visual effect possible.

Most fans concentrate on the jumps, and they're still the most important. All the top male skaters in the world have mastered all six triple jumps. Several now also have a quadruple jump. As well, they can combine these triples with other triple and double jumps. The top women skaters can do all the triples except the triple Axel, both alone and in combination with double jumps.

"You definitely have to put the jumps in the right place in the program," says Uschi Keszler. She is the choreographer for Elvis Stojko, Brasseur and Eisler, and several other top skaters.

"The music will tell you which jump should go where. An edge jump is a lot more powerful than a toe jump. It usually goes with more dramatic music. You might use a Salchow out of circular steps, which could be softer music. Or, if you have a jump that is weaker than another, you might use it as a fill-in. You don't put it at a dramatic point in the music because the skater might not make it, ruining the whole program."

The hardest jumps are almost always scheduled early in the program. This is for two reasons: so the skater isn't tired when they're attempted, and so the skater doesn't spend all the early part of the program worrying about them.

After the jumps are in place, the other elements are added to the program. Spins are planned for visual effect. Footwork is laid out to connect jumps and spins and to demonstrate the speed of the skater and sometimes for a little rest period between harder elements.

Once the elements are in order, the program has been designed in its roughest form. Then the real training starts, in July and August. While their friends are out swimming, boating, and getting a suntan, skaters are in cold arenas. They are trying triple Axels time and again, falling time and again. Skaters practice five or six hours a day during this period. They do the jumps and spins and footwork on their own. They do bits of their program several times each practice. And they perform complete run-throughs of their programs a couple of times.

Little by little the finished product takes shape. Adjustments are made if it's too hard in some parts, too easy in others. As skaters become more familiar with their program they add little nods of the head, dips of the knees, and flicks of the wrists, to make their performance more pleasing to the eye. Those little artistic additions are what can make the difference when skaters reach the upper levels of their sport.

The jumps

It's no wonder figure skaters see the world differently than most other athletes do. They spend most of their time going backward!

"It's funny," says Kurt Browning. "Just recently I started working on my forward skating more. I realized it wasn't strong enough because we do go backward so much — I'd say about 65 percent of the time or so. You go backward because you can cut a larger swath of ice. That means you can get your legs farther

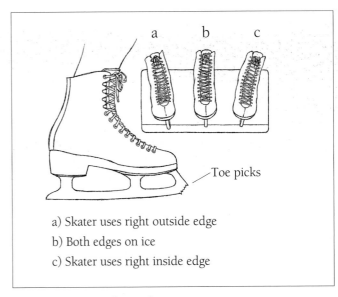

a) Skater uses right outside edge
b) Both edges on ice
c) Skater uses right inside edge

How skaters use their edges.

apart and get more power from pulling than from pushing, like you do going forward."

The power and speed generated by backward skating are needed to help lift the skater into the sport's most spectacular sight: the jumps.

Most skaters jump and spin counter-clockwise. But a few — such as Canada's legendary classical artist Toller Cranston and 16-year-old German sensation Tanja Szewczenko — perform their elements with a clockwise rotation.

As many as 47 jumps and jump variations are listed in most rule books. However, almost all of them start with some form of the six basic jumps: the toe loop, the Salchow, the flip, the loop, the Lutz, and the Axel. Three of those (the Axel, Salchow, and Lutz) are named for the skaters who either invented or perfected them. The other three are descriptions of how the jump looks.

Jumps are most important in men's and women's singles skating, but pairs use them too. Side-by-side jumps are key elements in pairs programs. The man and woman must be able to do them at the same height, at the same speed and, most importantly, at the same time. Also, pairs have "throws." These are really jumps by the woman in which the takeoff is assisted by the man "throwing" her. She must, of course, take care of the landing herself. Ice dancers don't do jumps. In fact, the rules forbid them.

Five factors separate the jumps from each other. These factors are: which foot is planted into the ice to lift the skater into the air; upon which foot the jump is landed; which edge of the skate blade is used in the takeoff; which edge is used in the landing; and whether the toe picks on the front of the skate are used to help the takeoff. The difficulty of the jump is determined by the number of rotations. For instance, a double Salchow is usually tougher than a single toe loop. If the number of rotations is the same, the Salchow and toe loop are considered the easiest two jumps. The Axel is the hardest because it is the only one that the skater enters facing forward. The Lutz is the second hardest. The flip and loop are somewhere in between. Difficulty performing the jumps may vary from skater to skater.

Both men and women have done triples of all six jumps. When it comes to quadruples, only the quadruple toe loop has been done in competition, and only by a few men. No woman has yet landed one in competition, but some are close.

The foot that pushes off the ice is called the "skating foot." The one that goes into the air first to help with the spinning motion is called the "free foot." After rotating, the skater comes down on the "landing foot." That can be either the original skating foot or the original free foot, depending upon the jump.

Single

AXEL

This jump is named after the Norwegian who invented it, Axel Paulsen. The Axel requires the skater to take off from the forward outside edge of the skating foot. The skater then performs one-and-a-half rotations in the air (or two-and-a-half for a double Axel or three-and-a-half for a triple Axel) and lands on the back outside edge of the free foot. There is an extra half-rotation, making this jump the most difficult to do, compared with other jumps.

Single

LUTZ

After Donald Jackson performed the first triple Lutz in 1963, there wasn't another one done at the World

Championships for another 11 years. It is a difficult, frightening jump. The skater needs a long glide to set it up and goes against the natural body movement. The jump is approached clockwise, but performed counter-clockwise. Using the toe pick on the free foot, the skater takes off from the back outside edge of the skating foot and lands on the back outside edge of the free foot.

Double

FLIP

The flip is the same as the Lutz, but it takes off from the back inside edge of the skating foot instead of the outside edge. It also uses the toe pick of the free foot for help and lands on the back outside edge of the free foot. The skates look as if they're flipping in the air.

Double

LOOP

The skater takes off from the back outside edge of the skating foot and lands on the back outside edge of the takeoff (skating) foot. The skates look as if they're forming a loop on the way into the air.

SALCHOW

Single

This jump is named after Ulrich Salchow, the Swede who won the first Olympic championship in 1908. The Salchow takes off from the back inside edge of the skating foot. It lands on the back outside edge of the free foot.

TOE LOOP

Double

Usually the first jump to be mastered is the toe loop in one of its many forms. The skater takes off from the back outside edge of the skating foot, with the help of the toe pick of the free foot. He or she lands on the back outside edge of the free foot. This jump is also called a "cherry." If there is a small turn (usually called a "three-turn") just before the jump, it's called a "toe-walley."

COMBINATION JUMPS

In a combination jump, the skater performs two jumps one after the other, with nothing in between. The skater lands the first jump on one foot, then uses that same foot to take off for the second jump. There can be no change of feet in between. In the technical program, one of the required elements is always a combination jump. Some women, such as Nancy Kerrigan, do triple-triple combinations. Most men can do at least one triple-triple.

JUMP SERIES

A jump series differs from a combination jump. Extra steps or turns or spins are taken between the jumps. A jump series is visually effective. Many skaters use one near the end of a program to show they still have speed, power, and stamina left.

Costumes plain and fancy

The outfit that a skater wears in competition is very important to the overall effect. It helps "sell" the idea to the audience and judges. If you want to skate to rock 'n' roll, you can't be dressed like a ballerina.

Even from their first years on blades, skaters are used to wearing costumes. In early competitions, the costumes are usually simple: skating skirts and tops for the girls, pants and tops for the boys. But most young skaters are members of skating clubs, and usually a club stages an annual carnival. The carnival is a youngster's first chance to perform in front of an audience. There are some skating solos, a few group numbers, and lots of fancy costumes. Many skaters first dressed up as a daffodil, a dancing bear, or a pixie in the club carnival.

The International Skating Union has some rules about costumes, however. They are not supposed to be too revealing or too theatrical. More and more, though, skaters are reaching beyond those restrictions.

At the upper level of world competition, costumes — like music — can be expensive. Many skaters, both men and women, wear freeskate costumes that can cost thousands of dollars. There were rumors that Surya Bonaly's outfit for the 1992 Olympics, made by a top Paris fashion designer, was worth $25,000. She wore special weights during practice to accustom herself to how heavy her freeskate costume was going to be.

Different skaters have different ideas about costuming. Many American and European skaters have designer-made outfits. But some have a local seamstress or family member make their outfits. Some skaters don't like glitter, others do. Austrian crystals are sometimes sewn into a costume to catch light and to sparkle. A box of 100 can cost $100, and several boxes might be needed.

But Canadian champion Josée Chouinard reminds young skaters: "Costumes are important as long as they fit you well and match your music and choreography. It's a total package. But if you don't have good music and good choreography and a good program, you can pay $20,000 and it won't make a difference."

Judging

Of all the parts making up figure skating, judging is the most difficult to understand.

Sometimes it looks as if the judges themselves don't understand what they're doing. Skating fans think one athlete should win. Instead, a different one captures the gold medal.

But judges are trained for years. They are selected because they are knowledgeable about all of figure skating's requirements. Some of these are very complicated and not easily seen by the average skating fan.

Skaters are not just judged upon how far, high, or fast they go, although those are all important. They are also marked on how well they perform each element in their program. They are marked on how well they present themselves to their audience, and whether their jumps, spins, and footwork match their music.

Because tastes differ, it would not be fair to have just one or two judges. So at major competitions such as the World Championships or Olympics, there are nine judges for each event. No country may have two judges for the same event. One judge's opinion counts just as much as another's.

Each judge gives each skater two marks. The first mark is for technical merit. This includes what elements are attempted, and how well each is performed. The second mark is for artistic impression. This evaluates such things as how interesting the program is, how well it fits the music, and how much of the ice surface is covered during the program.

The maximum is 6.0 but decimals, such as 5.8, are used. Once a judge determines the two marks, they are added together to rank the skaters. How high the marks are from one judge to another is not important. The only thing that matters is the order in which the judge ranks that skater.

For instance, in the example given below, Judge One gave Skater A 5.9 for technical merit and 5.7 for artistic impression. Skater A's total, then, was 11.6 (5.9 + 5.7).

Judge One liked Skater C's artistic work better than Skater A's but felt Skater A was better technically. So Skater C's marks were 5.8 and 5.9, which add up to 11.7. But Skater B, the judge thought, was equal to Skater A in technical (5.9) and to Skater C in artistry (5.9), so her marks added together total 11.8, higher than both her opponents.

On Judge One's card, then, Skater B would finish first, Skater C second, and Skater A third. Every judge does the same addition for every skater. Whichever skater has the most first-place votes wins the competition. Whichever has the most second-place votes finishes second, and so on.

It would appear in the example that Judge Two marked Skater B lower than Judge One, since the total is only 10.9. But that judge also marked the other skaters lower than Judge One did. Judge Two, in fact, ranked the three skaters in exactly the same order as the other judge and that's all that counts.

Remember, it's *not* whether one judge marks a skater *higher* than another judge marks that skater. What's important is the *order* in which each judge ranks each skater.

	Technical	Artistic	Total	Rank
Judge One				
Skater A	5.9	5.7	11.6	3
Skater B	5.9	5.9	11.8	1
Skater C	5.8	5.9	11.7	2
Judge Two				
Skater A	5.6	5.1	10.7	3
Skater B	5.5	5.4	10.9	1
Skater C	5.4	5.4	10.8	2

Why do skaters skate?

Besides all the time on the ice, skaters spend at least two hours a day training off the ice. One day, it might be working with a dance coach to increase flexibility and artistry. Another day they might be in the gym working on the strength and stamina required to get through long, demanding programs.

"Yeah, it's work. It's very hard work, but there is no substitute for it," says Elvis Stojko's coach, Doug Leigh. "You have to put those hours in."

Why do they do it? The simple answer, given by almost every good skater, is that they love the sport. Otherwise, it would be impossible to drag yourself to the arena day after day. You can't give up all the free time that your non-skating friends have unless you have a deep passion for the feel of a boot on your foot and your blade on the ice.

There are a variety of reasons that the world's top skaters got into their sport. Oksana Baiul was turned down when she wanted to study ballet, so her grandfather bought her a pair of skates instead. Elvis Stojko's parents say that, when he was three years old, he saw a skater on TV doing a spin. He said, "I wanna do dat!"

Like Elvis, many skaters were stimulated to skate by seeing others before them. Kristi Yamaguchi was inspired by Dorothy Hamill. Kristi herself is probably the reason many young American girls started to skate. Brian Orser, the first Canadian in 24 years to win a gold medal, saw 1962 world champion Don Jackson in an ice show. That "really got me going," he reports.

But today's stars all agree upon this: the most important thing is to get pleasure out of skating. That's the advice they want to pass on to young skaters.

"Make sure that you always enjoy it," says Isabelle Brasseur. "And you should know that there will be times when it gets rough and you want to quit. But you have to stick with it. You have to find out what you enjoy about skating and that will help you get through the parts that are very tough."

OLYMPIC GOLD MEDAL WINNERS

MEN
1908 Ulrich Salchow (Sweden)
1920 Gillis Grafström (Sweden)
1924 Gillis Grafström (Sweden)
1928 Gillis Grafström (Sweden)
1932 Karl Schäfer (Austria)
1936 Karl Schäfer (Austria)
1948 Dick Button (U.S.A.)
1952 Dick Button (U.S.A.)
1956 Hayes Jenkins (U.S.A.)
1960 David Jenkins (U.S.A.)
1964 Manfred Schnelldorfer (Germany)
1968 Wolfgang Schwarz (Austria)
1972 Ondrej Nepela (Czechoslovakia)
1976 John Curry (Great Britain)
1980 Robin Cousins (Great Britain)
1984 Scott Hamilton (U.S.A.)
1988 Brian Boitano (U.S.A.)
1992 Viktor Petrenko (Unified Team)
1994 Alexei Urmanov (Russia)

WOMEN
1908 Madge Syers (Great Britain)
1920 Magda Julin-Mauroy (Sweden)
1924 Herma Plank-Szabo (Austria)
1928 Sonja Henie (Norway)
1932 Sonja Henie (Norway)
1936 Sonja Henie (Norway)
1948 Barbara Ann Scott (Canada)
1952 Jeannette Altwegg (Great Britain)
1956 Tenley Albright (U.S.A.)
1960 Carol Heiss (U.S.A.)
1964 Sjoukje Dijkstra (Netherlands)
1968 Peggy Fleming (U.S.A.)
1972 Beatrix Schuba (Austria)
1976 Dorothy Hamill (U.S.A.)
1980 Anett Pötzsch (East Germany)
1984 Katarina Witt (East Germany)
1988 Katarina Witt (East Germany)
1992 Kristi Yamaguchi (U.S.A.)
1994 Oksana Baiul (Ukraine)

PAIRS
1908 Anna Hubler; Heinrich Burger (Germany)
1920 Ludowika Eilers; Walter Jakobsson (Finland)
1924 Helene Engelmann; Alfred Berger (Austria)
1928 Andrée Joly; Pierre Brunet (France)
1932 Andrée Brunet; Pierre Brunet (France)
1936 Maxi Herber; Ernst Baier (Germany)
1948 Micheline Lannoy; Pierre Baugniet (Belgium)
1952 Ria Falk; Paul Falk (Germany)
1956 Sissy Schwartz; Kurt Oppelt (Austria)
1960 Barbara Wagner; Robert Paul (Canada)
1964 Ludmila Belousova; Oleg Protopopov (Soviet Union)
1968 Ludmila Protopopov; Oleg Protopopov (Soviet Union)
1972 Irina Rodnina; Alexei Ulanov (Soviet Union)
1976 Irina Rodnina; Aleksandr Zaitsev (Soviet Union)
1980 Irina Rodnina; Aleksandr Zaitsev (Soviet Union)
1984 Elena Valova; Oleg Vasiliev (Soviet Union)
1988 Ekaterina Gordeeva; Sergei Grinkov (Soviet Union)
1992 Natalia Mishkutienok; Artur Dmitriev (Unified Team)
1994 Ekaterina Gordeeva; Sergei Grinkov (Russia)

ICE DANCE
1976 Ludmila Pakhomova; Aleksandr Gorshkov (Soviet Union)
1980 Natalia Linichuk; Gennadi Karponosov (Soviet Union)
1984 Jayne Torvill; Christopher Dean (Great Britain)
1988 Natalia Bestemianova; Andrei Bukin (Soviet Union)
1992 Marina Klimova; Sergei Ponomarenko (Unified Team)
1994 Oksana Gritschuk; Evgeny Platov (Russia)

Index